Fully W

written by **Ellen Warwick** ✱ illustrated by **Bernice Lum**

Kids Can Press

For Stacey, who got the ball rolling — EW

For miss alex arnott. Not only can she "knit one" heck of a scarf, she's also a very talented designer and artist who cooks a mean pot roast and "purls, too" — BL

pLanet girL™ is a trademark of Kids Can Press Ltd.

Text © 2007 Ellen Warwick
Illustrations © 2007 Bernice Lum

Kids Can Press acknowledges the financial support of the Government of Ontario, through the Ontario Media Development Corporation's Ontario Book Initiative, and the Government of Canada, through the BPIDP, for our publishing activity.

Published in Canada by
Kids Can Press Ltd.
29 Birch Avenue
Toronto, ON M4V 1E2

Published in the U.S. by
Kids Can Press Ltd.
2250 Military Road
Tonawanda, NY 14150

www.kidscanpress.com

Edited by Yvette Ghione
Designed by Karen Powers and Marie Bartholomew
Printed and bound in China

CM 07 0 9 8 7 6 5 4 3 2 1

Library and Archives Canada Cataloguing in Publication

Warwick, Ellen
    Fully woolly / written by Ellen Warwick;
illustrated by Bernice Lum.

(Planet girl)
ISBN 978-1-55337-798-6 (bound)

1. Knitting—Juvenile literature. 2. Crocheting—Juvenile literature. 3. Felt work—Juvenile literature. I. Lum, Bernice II. Title. III. Series.

TT820.W284 2007   j746.43   C2007-901120-9

Kids Can Press is a Corus™ Entertainment company

Contents

HEY, YARN GIRL!

Tired of wearing the SAME OLD shopping mall DUDS as everyone else you know? Don't want to be a sheep anymore? Ready to show your own SASSY STYLE? Get set to get SHEEP CHIC!

What can you knit with two sticks and a piece of string? What can't *you* KNIT?! *Once you've learned the two basic stitches — knit and purl — it's a* WILD *and* WOOLLY *world of possibilities. Check inside this book for* COOL *twists on the usual suspects like* HATS *and* SCARVES. *Plus you'll find some* EYE-POPPING *stuff like woolly* ART *to wow up your walls and knitted* BAUBLES *to add some dash to your panache.*

But knitting's just the beginning! Try your hand at some COOL CROCHET. It takes no time to learn the basics: you'll soon be on your crochet way. There's no looking back once you've whipped up an EASY and OH-SO-MOD choker or 70s-inspired circle bag.

Or, if you're a little needle-shy, try the two kinds of FELTING in here, which take wool fiber from FLUFF to FABULOUS. Why not give a wickedly cool woven scarf or some WOW-INSPIRING wall art a whirl? No knitting needles required!

So c'mon — join the NEEDLECRAFT REVOLUTION! Start flipping the pages to find all the stuff you'll need to get clicking (and hooking and needling) — easy-to-understand patterns, the basics of yarn know-how and handy TIPS and TRICKS to keep it SIMPLE and FUN.

HOLD ON!

Don't miss this section! There's tons of important information here!

Before You Get the Sticks Clicking

Never knitted or crocheted before? Even though most of the projects in here are easy-peasy, it's a good idea to practice a little first before you tackle them. Check out the back of the book for handy how-tos, hints and tricks, and ask a friend, relative or neighbor to help you get started with the basics. If you don't have a pal who knows how to do needlework, try looking it up on the Internet, or pop down to your local yarn shop and ask one of the experts there.

ANATOMY OF A WOOL SHOP

Ever been to ewe-topia? Most yarn shops are packed to the rafters with mounds of gorgeous, delicious yarn. It's inspiring for sure, but it can be a bit overwhelming, too. Where to start? What to try? First thing to do is bring this book with you and ask for help. The shopkeeper will be happy to help you pick the right yarn and needles so your project will turn out just right. They'll have you in stitches in no time!

YARN IS JUST YARN, RIGHT? NOT QUITE!

Yarn can be made from all kinds of materials, but there are two main types: natural fiber yarn and synthetic yarn. Some natural ones, like wool, cashmere and alpaca, are made from animal fur. (Don't worry, it's just a haircut!) Other natural yarns, like cotton and linen, are made from plants, and silk is made from fibers spun by silkworms. Synthetic yarn is made of man-made stuff like acrylic and polyester. Whichever type of yarn you choose, the most important thing to remember is to get the right weight.

You'll notice that all the yarns in this book are described by weight — like worsted weight or chunky weight. "Weight" refers to how thick or thin the yarn is. When you buy your yarn, make sure you're getting the weight the project calls for. If it's thinner, your project will be way too small. If it's thicker, your project will be way too big. And wouldn't that be a drag?!

Knit Bit

WOOL = sheep

MOHAIR = angora goat

ANGORA = rabbit

CASHMERE = cashmere goat

ALPACA = alpaca, a relative of the llama

SILK = silkworm cocoon fiber

COTTON = cotton plant fiber

LINEN = flax plant fiber

So what the heck is gauge?

Well, for a small, five-letter word, gauge is definitely a big deal. "Gauge" refers to how tight or loose your knitting is. Usually gauge is measured by the number of stitches across the number of rows a 10 cm x 10 cm (4 in. x 4 in.) knitted or crocheted square will have. All balls of yarn have their gauge listed on the label — check to make sure it's the same as what's in the pattern. Like the yarn's weight, it's really important that your gauge matches the gauge in the pattern — if not, the project won't be the right size.

Always knit or crochet a gauge swatch — a small test piece of knitting or crocheting that has the same number of stitches and rows as the gauge. Then, measure the swatch to make sure it's 10 cm x 10 cm (4 in. x 4 in.). If it's too big, try using slightly smaller needles or hooks and work another swatch. If it's too small, use slightly larger needles or hooks. This is super important for hats, mittens, sweaters and other things where fit matters. It isn't as important for things like bags and scarves where it won't matter so much if they're a little bigger or smaller.

Knit Bit

What to do with all those pesky gauge swatches? How about sticking them onto the front of a gift card — especially when the gift is something you made out of the same yarn?! Or, sew them in half and stuff them with polyester filling and some catnip — perfect presents for your fave feline! You could also sew a bunch together in a strip to make a one-of-a-kind, never-to-be-copied hair band, belt or wristband.

TOOLS OF THE TRADE

Knitting needles and crochet hooks come in different sizes. Make sure you get the same size the project calls for or, just like with the yarn weight and gauge, your project won't come out right. Needle and hook sizes can be in millimeters (mm) or in U.S. sizes. Here are some handy charts that show you which millimeter size is the same as which U.S. size.

Scissors, seaming pins, a yarn needle, a tape measure, stitch markers and a felting needle are other things you'll definitely need before you get going.

Knitting Needle Sizes	
Metric	**U.S. Size**
2.25 mm	U.S. 1
2.75 mm	U.S. 2
3.25 mm	U.S. 3
3.5 mm	U.S. 4
3.75 mm	U.S. 5
4 mm	U.S. 6
4.5 mm	U.S. 7
5 mm	U.S. 8
5.5 mm	U.S. 9
6 mm	U.S. 10
6.5 mm	U.S. 10½
8 mm	U.S. 11
9 mm	U.S. 13
10 mm	U.S. 15
12.75 mm	U.S. 17
15 mm	U.S. 19
19 mm	U.S. 35
25 mm	U.S. 50

Crochet Hook Sizes	
Metric	**U.S. Size***
2.25 mm	B-1
2.75 mm	C-2
3.25 mm	D-3
3.5 mm	E-4
3.75 mm	F-5
4 mm	G-6
4.5 mm	7
5 mm	H-8
5.5 mm	I-9
6 mm	J-10
6.5 mm	K-10½
8 mm	L-11
9 mm	M/N-13
10 mm	N/P-15
15 mm	P/Q
16 mm	Q
19 mm	S

✱ *The letter or number may vary. Go by the millimeter (mm) sizing.*

WHAT'S WITH THE PROJECTS' PAGE NUMBER COLORS?

These colored page numbers tell you how difficult each project is.

BEGINNER

EASY

INTERMEDIATE

It's a good idea to start with the projects geared to your skill level and then work your way up as you get more practice. That way, you won't get frustrated — it's all about having loads of fun while making things you love!

RSF, WSF, RSTOG, WSTOG

RSF = Right side facing. The right side, or good side of the project, faces you.

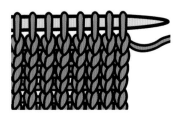

WSF = Wrong side facing. The wrong side, or underside of the project, faces you.

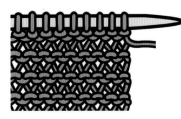

RSTOG = Right sides together. The right sides of two pieces of a project are placed together.

WSTOG = Wrong sides together. The wrong sides of two pieces of a project are placed together.

One last little thing ...

All yarn has a dye lot. A what lot? When yarn is dyed a color, it's done in batches. The batches are typically slightly different from one another. Make sure that all the yarn for your project is from the same dye lot — check out the number printed on the label — so that your yarn is all exactly the same color. Also, it's a really good idea to buy a little more yarn than you need, in case you make a mistake or run out.

Okay, one more last little thing ... Sometimes yarn comes in a skein, which means it's not wound into a ball. So, before you start knitting or crocheting, wind it into a ball.

color
4
Dye Lot
1736

WOOLLY
wools

Wild & Woolly

Ready to make some woolly magic by turning sticks and string into things to wear, things to carry and things to give? Make sure you get all the stuff you'll need together before you start.

 Knitting and crocheting are great to do curled up in your favorite chair, but the fab thing about these hobbies is that they're portable and sociable!

 Take your project on the bus, train or in the car. It's a great way to make a long trip way more fun — and productive, too!

 Take it to the beach, to the park or to the big game — no need to sit inside on a gorgeous day.

Join a knitting or crocheting group and share your funky ideas with other people who are passion-knit, too.

 Throw a knitting party! Make the invitations with paper and yarn and decorate your space with yarn streamers. They'll be mad about ewe!

Gumball necklace

Wool fiber is the stuff that comes after the sheep but before the yarn — it's the stuff that's spun into yarn. If you can't get the colors you love, buy some undyed and dye it yourself!

- Tear off a small amount of wool fiber, enough to roll into a ball about the size of a Ping-Pong ball.

- Follow the soapy-water felting directions on page 79.

- Repeat to make about 15 beads.

- When the beads are completely dry, thread the ribbon onto the yarn needle. Tie a knot about 25 cm (10 in.) from the end of the ribbon.

- Push the needle through one side of one bead and out the other. Slide the bead down the ribbon to the knot. Tie another knot close to the other side of the bead.

- Continue adding beads and knots until all the beads are strung. Tie your necklace around your neck with a small bow at the back.

Knit Bit

To make multicolored beads, take small pieces of different colored wool fiber and roll them into separate balls. Press the balls together and then continue with the directions on page 79.

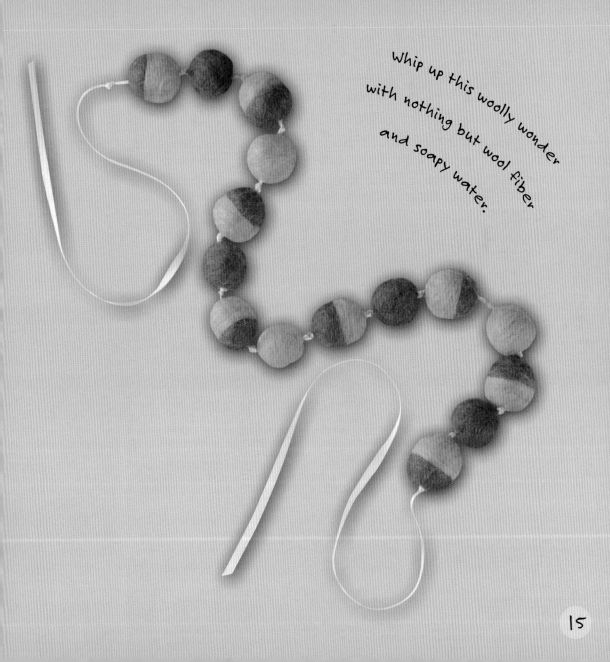

Whip up this woolly wonder with nothing but wool fiber and soapy water.

Punchy pouch

This punchy pouch can carry pens and pencils, lip gloss, cell phone, knitting or crocheting must-haves ... whatever!

BAG

- Make a slipknot and chain (ch, see page 74) 22.

- Then:
  Row 1: Starting at the second chain from the hook, single crochet (sc, see page 75) 20 stitches (sts), then ch 1. Turn.
  Row 2: Sc 20, ch 1. Turn. Repeat until your work measures 20 cm (8 in.).

- Fasten off (see page 77).

- Fold the bottom edge up to the top edge. Pin and then sew the side edges together with the yarn needle and yarn, removing the pins as you go.

- Weave in the ends and trim.

- one 50 g (1¾ oz.) ball of chunky weight yarn
- 6.5 mm (K-10½) crochet hook
- 18 cm (7 in.) zipper
- a sewing needle, and thread to match the zipper
- a small piece of cardboard
- a ruler or measuring tape, scissors, pins, a yarn needle

Gauge: 12 sts and 8 rows = 10 cm x 10 cm (4 in. x 4 in.)

- Open the zipper. Pin one zipper edge to an inside top edge of the pouch. With the sewing needle and thread, sew along the pinned zipper edge on the inside of the pouch, removing the pins as you go. Repeat to sew the other zipper edge to the other top edge of the pouch.

Add some pow to your purse with this eye-popping pouch!

POM-POM

- Draw a 5 cm (2 in.) circle onto cardboard. Cut it out. Then draw a 1 cm (½ in.) circle in the center of the first circle and cut it out to make a donut. Repeat.

- Place the two cardboard donuts together. Wind the yarn through the center hole and round and round the cardboard evenly until the center hole is almost filled up.

- Poke scissors through the yarn between the two cardboard circles. Cut the yarn around the outside edge of the circle, keeping the scissors between the cardboard the entire time.

- Cut a 30 cm (12 in.) piece of yarn. Fold it in half and then tie it around the pom-pom between the two pieces of cardboard. Separate the ends and wrap them around the pom-pom again. Tie a tight knot and remove the cardboard.

- Trim the pom-pom to make it even and round.

- With the yarn needle and yarn, sew the pom-pom to the zipper pull with a few long stitches. Tie a knot and trim the ends.

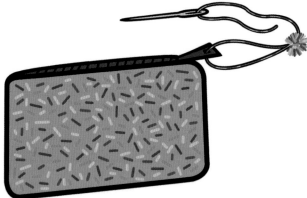

Woven wonder scarf

Whip up this easy weave in a snap. The secret to this super-simple craft is to use wool that is spun very loosely. That way the fibers can felt together.

- Cut ten 2 m (6 ft.) pieces of brown yarn.

- On a clean work surface, spread the brown yarn pieces 1 cm (½ in.) apart, lining up the ends. Stick a piece of masking tape across the yarn pieces 25 cm (10 in.) from one end.

- Starting just below the tape and leaving a 10 cm (4 in.) end, weave the pink yarn under the first brown yarn piece and over the second, under the third and over the fourth. Continue weaving under and over the brown yarn pieces.

- At the end of the row, weave back under the tenth brown yarn piece to start a new row. Continue weaving the second row so that the wool weaves opposite to the way it did on the first row. At the end of the row, slide the yarn up so that it's about 1 cm (½ in.) from the row above.

STUFF YOU NEED

- one 100 g (3½ oz.) ball of pink single-ply roving bulky weight yarn
- one 100 g (3½ oz.) ball of brown single-ply roving bulky weight yarn
- an iron and an ironing board, a thin piece of cloth
- a ruler or measuring tape, scissors, masking tape

- Continue weaving, adjusting the rows as you go, till you're 25 cm (10 in.) from the untaped ends of the brown yarn pieces.

- Tie the end of the pink yarn and the ends of the closest two brown yarn end pieces together with a single knot. Trim the pink yarn close to the knot. Tie the remaining eight brown yarn pieces together two at a time with single knots.

- Remove the masking tape from the other end of the scarf and repeat the last step.

- Cut eight 30 cm (12 in.) pieces of pink yarn. Fold one piece in half and push it through the hole between two brown yarn knots. Pull the pink yarn ends through the loop and tighten the knot. Repeat between the rest of the brown yarn knots on both ends of the scarf.

- Lay the scarf on an ironing board and cover it with a thin piece of cotton cloth. With an adult's help, set the iron to a high steam setting and, using the steam surge button, iron the scarf gently one section at a time until the fibers are flat and slightly felted together. Let cool.

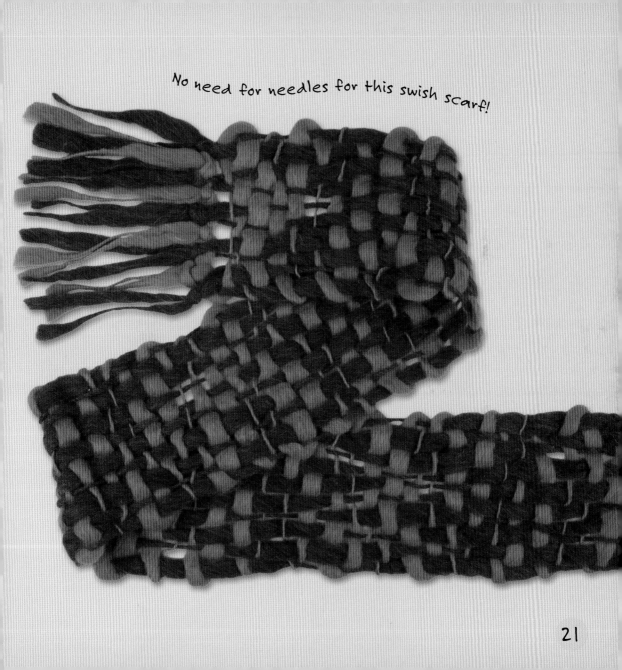

No need for needles for this swish scarf!

Knitty necklace

You'll look nifty in this ewe–nique necklace!

- With the brown yarn, cast on (CO, see page 66) 6 sts.

- Starting with a purl row, work 13 rows in stockinette stitch (St st, see page 69).

- Bind off (BO, see page 72).

- Thread one of the yarn ends onto the yarn needle. Sewing the short ends together using duplicate stitch (see page 73), make a tube.

- Slip a 16 mm (⅝ in.) wooden bead inside the knitted tube so that the bead holes are showing at each end of the tube.

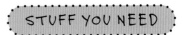

STUFF YOU NEED

- one 50 g (1¾ oz.) ball of brown double knit (DK) weight yarn
- one 50 g (1¾ oz.) ball of gold DK weight yarn
- one 50 g (1¾ oz.) ball of turquoise DK weight yarn
- 4 mm (U.S. 6) knitting needles
- six 16 mm (⅝ in.) round wood beads*
- 1 m (1 yd.) brown round leather lace
- about fifty 7 mm (⅓ in.) round metal spacers*
- about sixty 6 mm (⅓ in.) round metal beads*
- about forty 5 mm (¼ in.) square wood beads*
- about thirty 1 cm (½ in.) round wood beads*
- a ruler or measuring tape, scissors, a yarn needle

Make sure you can thread the beads and spacers onto the leather lace.

Gauge: 22 sts and 28 rows = 10 cm x 10 cm (4 in. x 4 in.)

What a wicked way to use up leftover scraps of wool!

These whip up in a flash and are perfect for gift giving.

- Thread one of the yarn ends onto the yarn needle. Weave the needle through the stitches at the tube end and draw them together, leaving an opening for the bead hole. Tie a knot and weave in the end. Repeat on the other end of the tube.

- Make another brown bead, then two gold and two turquoise beads the same way.

- Tie a knot in one end of the leather lace. Thread the wood and knitted beads and the metal beads and spacers on as shown.

- Undo the knot at the end of the lace and then tie the two ends together.

Baa baa bangles

STUFF YOU NEED

- about ½ ball of yarn (any weight)
- double-pointed knitting needles (dpn) the correct size for the yarn you use
- a ruler or measuring tape, scissors, a yarn needle

Got any leftover yarn? Don't hide it away in the back of a closet or drawer. These are a fab way to use it up and show it off!

- To figure out the length of the finished bracelet, measure around your wrist and add 2.5 cm (1 in.).

- CO 5 sts for thick wool or 7 sts for thinner wool.

- Knit one row. Instead of turning your work, slide the sts to the other end of the dpn. Repeat until the I-cord is the length you want. BO.

- With a yarn needle, sew the I-cord ends together, making sure that the bracelet is not twisted. Weave in the ends and trim.

Knit Bit

I-cord is just a small tube of stockinette stitch knitting. If you don't have double-pointed needles, simply slip the sts from the right needle back to the left one, keeping the right side facing you, before knitting the next row. It takes a bit longer, but it works just as well.

25

Rockin' ruched scarf

"Ruched" is just another word for gathered. The ruching in this scarf creates a ruffle effect in the middle instead of along the edge. Looks hard, but it's super easy. The trick? This scarf is knit sideways.

- With olive yarn, CO 160 sts.

- Work 11 rows in garter stitch (g st, see page 69).

- Next row, increase (inc) in every st by knitting and purling into the same st (kf&b, see page 70). You will have 320 sts on the needle.

- Switch to raspberry yarn (see page 71) and work 13 rows in stockinette stitch (St st, see page 69).

- Switch to olive yarn and knit two sts together (k2tog, see page 69) across the entire row. You will have 160 sts on the needle.

- Knit 11 rows in g st. BO.

- Weave in all the yarn ends.

STUFF YOU NEED

- two 25 g (⅞ oz.) balls of olive worsted weight yarn
- two 25 g (⅞ oz.) balls of raspberry worsted weight yarn
- 5.5 mm (U.S. 9) circular knitting needles
- a ruler or measuring tape, scissors, a yarn needle

Gauge: 18 sts and 24 rows = 10 cm x 10 cm (4 in. x 4 in.)

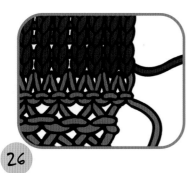

This tricky-looking scarf is actually a cinch to make.

Cheeky choker

Show your sassy style with this traffic-stopper!

- Leaving a 50 cm (20 in.) yarn end, make a slipknot. Ch 3.

- Row 1: Sc in the second and third chains from the hook. Ch 1. Turn. Repeat this pattern until your work measures 15 cm (6 in.).

- To add the bead, insert the hook into its center. Wrap the yarn around the hook once and then pull the bead through the loop on the hook. Ch 1. Wrap the yarn around the chains above the bead a few times.

- To make the other side of the choker, continue sc 2 sts in each row, followed by ch 1, as in Row 1, until both sides are the same length.

- Fasten off, leaving a 50 cm (20 in.) yarn end.

- Cut a 100 cm (40 in.) piece of yarn. Fold the yarn in half and use the crochet hook to pull the folded end through the edge of one end of the choker, then pull the ends through the loop. Braid the three yarn ends for about 30 cm (12 in.), then tie a knot and trim the ends.

- Repeat the last step to make another braid on the other end of the choker. Tie the choker around your neck with a bow at the back.

- one 50 g (1¾ oz.) ball of brown worsted weight cotton yarn
- 5 mm (H-8) crochet hook
- 3.5 cm (1½ in.) stone bead*
- a ruler or measuring tape, scissors, a yarn needle

Make sure you can thread the bead onto the crochet hook.

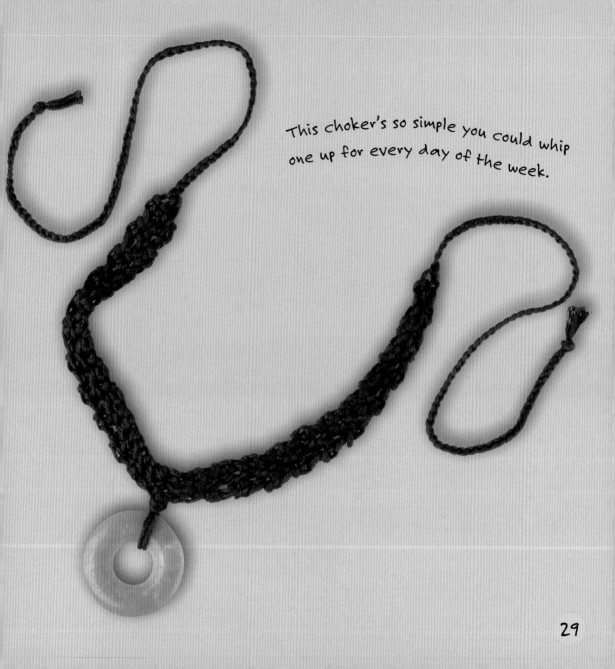

This choker's so simple you could whip one up for every day of the week.

29

Beaded beauty bracelet

Bedeck your get-up with a beaded bijou. It's definitely cheaper than the real stuff, and a lot cuter, too!

- Cut a 15 cm (6 in.) piece of thread and thread the sewing needle. Tie the thread ends around the yarn about 8 cm (3 in.) from the yarn end.

- Thread the beads onto the sewing needle and slide them down onto the yarn in this pattern: pink, green, pink, green, pink, green, pink. Repeat this pattern, sliding all the beads down far enough so that you have about 1 m (1 yd.) of yarn above the beads to work with. Remove the sewing needle and thread.

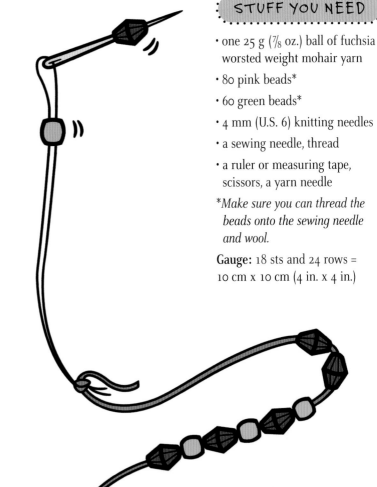

STUFF YOU NEED

- one 25 g (⅞ oz.) ball of fuchsia worsted weight mohair yarn
- 80 pink beads*
- 60 green beads*
- 4 mm (U.S. 6) knitting needles
- a sewing needle, thread
- a ruler or measuring tape, scissors, a yarn needle

Make sure you can thread the beads onto the sewing needle and wool.

Gauge: 18 sts and 24 rows = 10 cm x 10 cm (4 in. x 4 in.)

No need for diamonds, dahling,
when you've got homemade sparkle.

31

- CO 10 sts.

- Then:

  Row 1: Knit.

  Row 2: To add beads to this row, slide them up the yarn one at a time close to the needle in this pattern: purl 2 (p2), slide a bead up (bead), p1, bead, p1, bead, p1, bead, p1, bead, p1, bead, p1, bead, p2. Repeat this pattern for nineteen more rows, until you have used all of the beads.

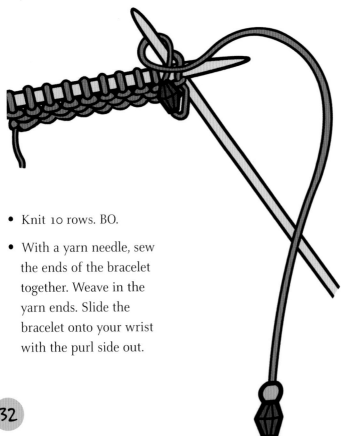

- Knit 10 rows. BO.

- With a yarn needle, sew the ends of the bracelet together. Weave in the yarn ends. Slide the bracelet onto your wrist with the purl side out.

Knit Bit

Personalize the pattern with different-colored beads or by not putting a bead between all of the stitches. Create a pattern on graph paper first (see Knitting charts, page 70) and then string the beads onto the wool, following your pattern back and forth across the rows. How about your name, a flower pattern or another design?

Sassy skullcap

Look smashing while you're dashing!

STUFF YOU NEED

• one 50 g (1¾ oz.) ball of orange worsted weight yarn

• one 50 g (1¾ oz.) ball of purple worsted weight yarn

• 5.5 mm (I-9) crochet hook

• stitch markers*

• a ruler or measuring tape, scissors, a yarn needle

*Use these to mark the beginning of each round.

Gauge: 16 sts and 10 rows = 10 cm x 10 cm (4 in. x 4 in.)

• With orange yarn, make a slipknot and ch 4. Ch 1 into the first chain to make a ring.

• Round (rnd) 1: Sc 8 sts into the ring. Join this rnd, and all of the rnds, with a sl st (see page 77) in the first st of the rnd.

• Rnd 2: Ch 1. Sc twice into every st. Join the rnd. You'll have 16 sts on the rnd.

• Rnd 3: Ch 1. Sc twice into the first and every other st. Join the rnd. You'll have 24 sts on the rnd.

• Rnd 4: Ch 3. Double crochet (dc, see page 76) twice into the first and every other st. Join the rnd. You'll have 36 sts on the rnd.

• Rnd 5: Ch 3. Dc twice into the first and every third st. Join the rnd. You'll have 48 sts on the rnd.

• Rnd 6: Ch 3. Dc twice into the first and every fourth st. Join the rnd. You'll have 60 sts on the rnd.

• Rnd 7 and 8: Ch 3. Dc every st. Join the rnd. You'll have 60 sts on the rnd.

• Rnd 9: Ch 3. Dc into the first and every sixth st. Join the rnd. You'll have 70 sts on the rnd.

• Rnd 10 to 15: Ch 3. Dc every st. Join the rnd. You'll have 70 sts on the rnd.

- Rnd 16: With purple yarn, ch 3. Dc into the third st. Dc in the next st. *Ch 1. Skip 1 st. Dc in the next two sts.* Repeat from * to * to the end of the rnd. Join the rnd.

- Rnd 17: *Ch 1. Sc through the arch below. Ch 3. Dc twice over the same arch below.* Repeat from * to * through each arch to the end of the rnd. Join the rnd.

- Fasten off.

Knit Bit

Flip this hat upside down and you've got a great container to hold hair doodads, loose change or any other little thing needing organizing. Use a sturdy yarn that's not too soft so that the bowl will stand upright.

This cap's so cute you won't want to wait for a chilly day to wear it!

Pixie hat

Keep the winter chills away with a perfectly adorable pixie hat. Useful and cute!

- two 50 g (1¾ oz.) balls of green chunky weight yarn
- one 50 g (1¾ oz.) ball of blue chunky weight yarn
- 8 mm (U.S. 11) knitting needles
- 8 mm (U.S. 11) double-pointed knitting needles (dpn)
- a ruler or measuring tape, scissors, pins, a yarn needle

Gauge: 12 sts and 16 rows = 10 cm x 10 cm (4 in. x 4 in.)

HAT

- With green yarn, CO 54 sts.
- Knit 13 cm (5 in.) in stockinette stitch (St st, see page 69).

Row 1: *K4, slip one knitwise (sl 1 k, see page 69), k1, then pass the slipped st over (psso, see page 69)*. Repeat from * to * eight times. You'll have 45 sts left on the needle.

Row 2: Purl.
Row 3: *K3, sl 1 k, k1, psso* eight times. You'll have 36 sts left on the needle.
Row 4: Purl.
Row 5: *K2, sl 1 k, k1, psso* eight times. You'll have 27 sts left on the needle.
Row 6: Purl.

Row 7: *K1, sl 1 k, k1, psso* eight times. You'll have 18 sts left on the needle.
Row 8: Purl.
Row 9: *Sl 1 k, k1, psso* eight times. You'll have 9 sts left on the needle.
Row 10: Purl.
Row 11: K1, k2tog four times. You'll have 5 sts left on the needle.

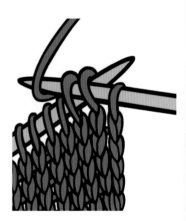

Row 12: Purl.
Row 13: K1, k2tog twice. You'll have 3 sts left on the needle.

Winter's much more fun when you've got a cozy hat to perk up your noggin.

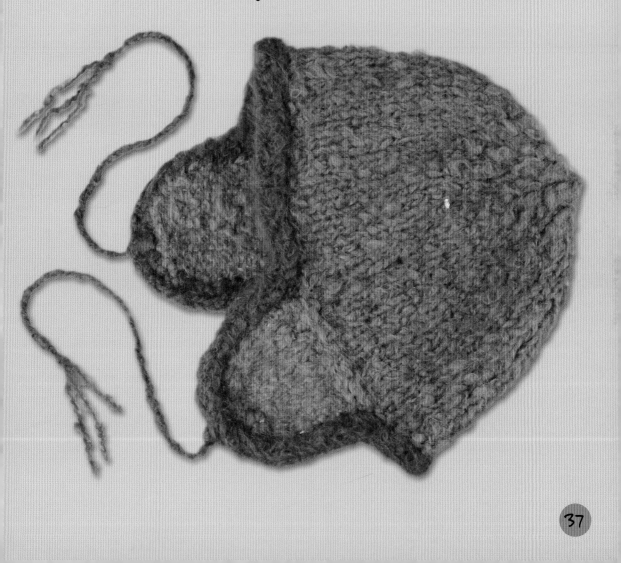

Row 14: P3tog. Break the wool and draw it through the last stitch, pulling the stitch closed.

- Pin, and then with yarn and a yarn needle, sew the side edges together to make a hat shape, removing the pins as you go. Weave in the ends.

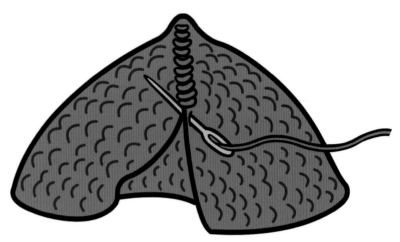

EARFLAPS: Make two

- With green yarn, CO 10 sts.
- Knit eight rows in St st.
  Row 9: K1, sl 1 k, k1, psso, k5, k2tog.
  Row 10: Purl.
  Row 11: K1, sl 1 k, k1, psso, k3, k2tog.
- BO, purlwise.

- Flatten the hat along the seam. Pin, and then with yarn and a yarn needle, sew one earflap to the center of the bottom edge of the hat, removing the pins as you go. Weave in the ends. Repeat to sew the second earflap.

I-CORD TRIM

- With blue yarn and dpn, CO 3 sts.

- Knit 1 row. Instead of turning your work, slide the sts to the other end of the dpn. Repeat until the I-cord measures 85 cm (34 in.).

- BO.

- Starting at the back seam of the hat, start pinning the I-cord around the edge of the hat and earflaps.

- With blue yarn and a yarn needle, sew the I-cord to the hat, removing the pins as you go.

EARFLAP TIES: Make two

- Cut three 40 cm (16 in.) pieces of blue yarn.

- Tie them together evenly with a knot at one end.

- Braid the yarn pieces, leaving about 7.5 cm (3 in.) free at the end. Tie another knot and trim the ends evenly.

- With blue yarn, sew one tie to the bottom of each earflap. Weave in the ends.

Knit Bit

Wanna keep it simple? Skip the earflaps and the ties and you'll have a hat in no time flat!

39

Tote-ally cool felted messenger bag

Find a couple of old sweaters at the local charity shop or in the back of your closet and felt them for a durable (and delightful!) bag for those heavy homework days.

STUFF YOU NEED

- two old, 100% wool pullover sweaters*

- a sewing machine or a sewing needle

- thread to match the sweaters

- an iron and an ironing board

- a mesh laundry bag, laundry detergent, a towel

- a ruler or measuring tape, a pencil, scissors, pins

Make sure the sweaters are 100% wool, or they won't felt properly.

- Follow the instructions on page 80 to felt the sweaters in the washine machine. Let dry.

- To make the base of the bag, start at the waistband of one sweater and measure, mark and cut out a 30 cm x 35 cm (12 in. x 14 in.) piece from the front of the sweater. Repeat on the back of the sweater. The waistband edge should measure 30 cm (12 in.).

Mix it up by using two different sweaters for the front and back of the bag.

- Place the sweater pieces RSTOG, lining up the waistband edges evenly. Pin along the three cut edges.

- Using small stitches about 0.5 cm (¼ in.) from the edges, sew around the three pinned edges, removing the pins as you go. Turn the bag right side out. Ask an adult to help you set the iron to medium-high heat to steam and flatten the seams.

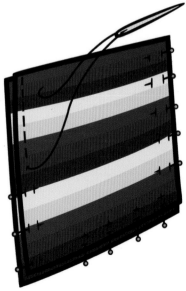

STRAP

- Use the measuring tape to figure out how long you want the strap to be. Add 2.5 cm (1 in.) to this measurement.

- Measure, mark and cut out a piece from one sweater sleeve that is 9 cm (3½ in.) wide and half the strap length measurement. Repeat on the other sleeve.

- Place the strap pieces RSTOG. Pin one short end of each of the straps together. Sew them together using small stitches about 0.5 cm (¼ in.) from the edge, removing the pins as you go.

- Open the strap up. Fold it in half lengthwise with RSTOG and pin. Sew along the pinned edge using small stitches about 0.5 cm (¼ in.) from the edge, removing the pins as you go.

- Turn the strap inside out. You can use a large knitting needle to help you poke it through.

- With an adult's help, steam and flatten the strap, arranging the seam in the middle of one side of the strap.

ALL TOGETHER

- Centering it over one side seam, pin and then sew one strap end to the top edge, removing the pins as you go. Repeat to sew the other end of the strap to the other side of the bag.

- To make the flap, start at the waistband of the second sweater and measure, mark and cut out a 25 cm x 20 cm (10 in. x 8 in.) piece from the back of the sweater. The waistband edge should measure 25 cm (10 in.).

- With RSTOG, line up the top edge of the bag with the longer cut edge of the flap evenly and pin.

- Sew along the pinned edge using small stitches about 0.5 cm (¼ in.) from the edge, removing the pins as you go. With an adult's help, steam and flatten the seam.

Knit Bit

Save the extra sweater bits and sew up a darling matching case to keep from losing your little necessities!

Chic circle bag

Carry your junk with some spunk in this saucy circle bag.

:·: STUFF YOU NEED :·:

- three 50 g (1¾ oz.) balls of bulky yarn
- 6.5 mm (K-10½) crochet hook
- two 15 cm (6 in.) bamboo purse handles
- stitch markers*
- a ruler or measuring tape, scissors, pins, a yarn needle

Use these to mark the beginning of each round.

Gauge: 8 sts and 6 rows = 10 cm x 10 cm (4 in. x 4 in.)

FRONT/BACK: Make two

- Make a slipknot and ch 4. Ch 1 into the first chain to make a ring.

- Rnd 1: Ch 3. Dc 11 sts into the ring. Join this rnd, and all of the rnds, with a sl st in the first st of the rnd.

- Rnd 2: Ch 3. Dc twice into every st. Join the rnd. You'll have 24 sts on the rnd.

- Rnd 3: Ch 3. Dc twice into the first and every second st. Join the rnd. You'll have 36 sts on the rnd.

- Rnd 4: Ch 3. Dc twice into the first and every third st. Join the rnd. You'll have 48 sts on the rnd.

- Rnd 5: Ch 3. Dc twice into the first and every fourth st. Join the rnd. You'll have 60 sts on the rnd.

- Rnd 6: Ch 3. Dc twice into the first and every fifth st. Join the rnd. You'll have 72 sts on the rnd.

- Rnd 7: Ch 3. Dc twice into the first and every sixth st. Join the rnd. You'll have 84 sts on the rnd. Join the rnd.

- Fasten off.

This circle's not vicious
— just delicious!

45

HANDLES

- Lay one crocheted circle WSF on a work surface. Place one handle about 5 cm (2 in.) below the top edge of the circle.

- Fold the top edge of the circle through the handle and pin.

- With yarn and a yarn needle, sew along the edge of the handle.

- Repeat with the other circle and handle.

ALL TOGETHER

- Place the two purse pieces together WSTOG and pin.

- Starting and ending about 20 cm (8 in.) from the bamboo handles, sew around the edge of the purse with a yarn needle and yarn, removing the pins as you go.

- Weave in the yarn ends and trim.

Knit Bit

Make a matching mini-case by stopping after a few rounds and adding snaps to close it.

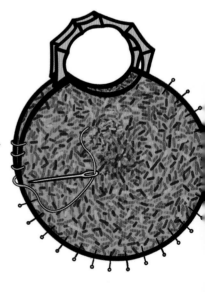

Woolly wall art

Who needs a Picasso when you've got custom art by you?

- Lay the felt on the upholstery foam.

- Measure and cut a few 40 cm (16 in.) pieces of turquoise wool fiber. Lay the pieces on the felt to make a thick layer. Cut more pieces of turquoise wool fiber as needed to cover the entire felt piece.

- Needle felt (see page 78) the wool fiber until it is completely felted and smooth.

- To make the design, flatten a piece of yellow fiber and cut out a circle that is about 5 cm (2 in.) across. Needle felt it to the left and a little above the center of the picture.

- a 40 cm x 40 cm (16 in. x 16 in.) piece of craft felt
- a 40 cm x 40 cm (16 in. x 16 in.) piece of 2.5 cm (1 in.) upholstery foam
- about 1 kg (2½ lb.) of turquoise wool fiber
- about 50 g (1¾ oz.) of yellow wool fiber
- about 50 g (1¾ oz.) of red wool fiber
- about 50 g (1¾ oz.) of dark turquoise fiber
- about 100 g (3½ oz.) of olive wool fiber
- a felting needle
- a 30 cm x 30 cm (12 in. x 12 in.) artist's framed canvas
- a glue gun and glue sticks
- a ruler or measuring tape, scissors

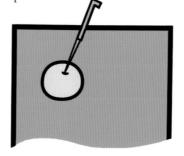

Repeat to add a red circle to the right of and lower than the yellow circle.

- Cut a strip of dark turquoise fiber and place it around the yellow circle. Needle felt it in place.

- Cut a strip of olive fiber and place it around the dark turquoise circle. Needle felt it in place.

- Remove the upholstery foam and lay the felted piece right side down on a clean work surface.

- Center the canvas right side down on the felted piece. With a glue gun, glue the edges of the felted piece to the back of the canvas.

Knit Bit

Why not create your own one-of-a-kind design instead? Plan it on paper first — let your fave colors inspire you!

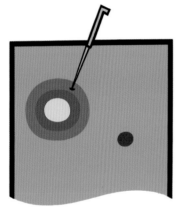

Repeat to make an olive circle around the red circle.

- Cut a strip of olive fiber and place it in a straight line down from a circle. Needle felt it in place. Repeat for the other circle.

Let dry. Ask an adult to help you hang your creation.

Add some woolly wow to your walls!

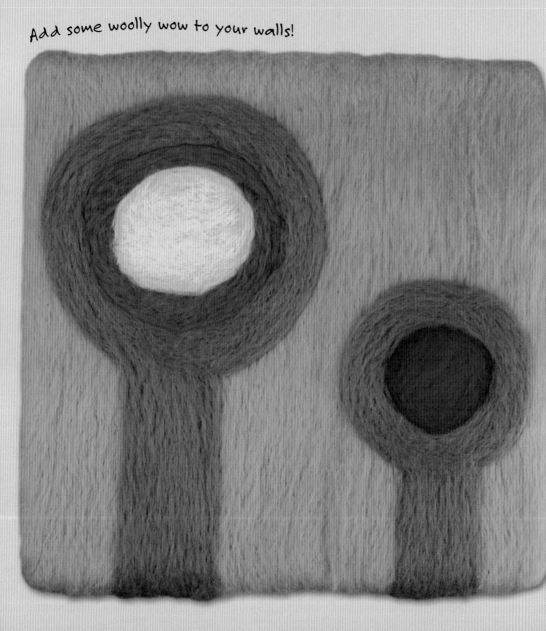

Felt-fabulous cushion

Add a little lounge appeal to your bedroom by tossing one or two of these cozy cushions on your bed.

STUFF YOU NEED

- one 50 g (1¾ oz.) ball of blue worsted weight yarn
- three 50 g (1¾ oz.) balls of brown worsted weight yarn
- one 50 g (1¾ oz.) ball of olive worsted weight yarn
- one 50 g (1¾ oz.) ball of orange worsted weight yarn
- one 50 g (1¾ oz.) ball of red worsted weight yarn
- 5.5 mm (U.S. 9) knitting needles
- a package of polyester stuffing
- a sewing needle and brown thread
- a mesh laundry bag, laundry detergent, a towel
- a ruler or measuring tape, scissors, a yarn needle, pins

Gauge

Before felting: 20 sts and 24 rows = 10 cm x 10 cm (4 in. x 4 in.)

After felting: 20 sts and 24 rows = 10 cm x 9 cm (4 in. x 3½ in.)

Finished size

Before felting: 30 cm x 35 cm (12 in. x 14 in.)

After felting: 30 cm x 30 cm (12 in. x 12 in.)

BACK

- With brown yarn, CO 60 sts.
- Work 79 rows in stockinette stitch (St st, see page 69).
- BO, purlwise. Weave in the ends.

FRONT

- With blue yarn, CO 60 sts.
- Work 79 rows in St st in this pattern: 8 blue, 3 brown, 5 olive, 4 orange, 10 red, 1 brown, 2 blue, 3 orange, 3 olive, 7 blue, 2 red, 6 brown, 6 orange, 1 blue, 3 olive, 1 red, 2 orange, 6 blue, 6 olive
- BO, purlwise. Weave in the ends.

A comfy cushion or two turns your bed into a cozy hangout for you and your pals.

FELTING

- Follow the directions on page 80 and agitate the front and back pieces in the washing machine for 25 to 30 minutes or until they're felted.

- Lay them on a towel and measure to make sure both pieces are 30 cm x 30 cm (12 in. x 12 in.). Gently pull them into shape if needed. Let dry, checking the measurements a few times and adjusting the shape again if needed.

ALL TOGETHER

- With WSTOG, pin the front and back together along three sides.

- Thread the sewing needle with a piece of thread about as long as your arm. Tie a double knot at the end of the thread.

- Starting at one corner, sew the front and back together with small overhand stitches along the three pinned sides, removing the pins as you go.

Knit Bit

Make a super-sized floor cushion by knitting four front squares and four back squares, felting them and then sewing them all together.

- Fill the pillow with polyester stuffing. Pin and then sew the open side closed, removing the pins as you go.

Yummy Yarn Stuff

Hooked yet? Check out this section if you want to get to the next level of yarn addiction — natty knitted accessories for your needlecraft habit. Look ahead for

a felted project journal to record all your brilliant ideas and inspiration in one fuzzy spot

a cheeky carryall bag that'll mean you never have to leave your yarn at home again

a swish needle case to keep your needles tucked away together in one compact and stylish spot

three great ways to add sensational style to your needles — no one will have a pair like 'em!

Funky felted journal

Just the thing to keep track of all your projects!

- CO 54 sts.

- Work in stockinette stitch (St st, see page 69) until your work measures 75 cm (30 in.).

- BO. Weave in the ends.

FELTING

- Follow the directions on page 80 and agitate your work in the washing machine for about five minutes or until it's felted.

- Lay it on a towel and measure to make sure it's the correct finished size. Gently pull it into shape if needed. Let dry, checking the measurements a few times and adjusting the shape again if needed.

STUFF YOU NEED

- two 100 g (3½ oz.) balls of medium green worsted weight yarn
- 4.5 mm (U.S. 7) knitting needles
- a sewing needle and green thread
- a drinking glass or small dish
- leftover scraps of yarn
- a 18 cm x 23 cm (7 in. x 9 in.) binder with a 2.5 cm (1 in.) wide spine
- a ruler or tape measure, scissors, a yarn needle, pins, a pencil or pen

Gauge

Before felting: 20 sts and 28 rows = 10 cm x 10 cm (4 in. x 4 in.)

After felting: 20 sts and 28 rows = 9 cm x 10 cm (3½ in. x 4 in.)

Finished size

Before felting: 27 cm x 75 cm (11 in. x 30 in.)

After felting: 25 cm x 63 cm (10 in. x 25 in.)

Take it personally and embroider your name or a title for your journal on the front cover.

Pop it into this beauty of a bag and keep your projects together on the go!

ALL TOGETHER

- With WSF, measure 13 cm (5 in.) from one corner along the long edge. Fold the short edge of the cover over at this measurement and pin it at the top and bottom edges to make a pocket.

- Thread the sewing needle with a piece of thread about as long as your arm. Tie a double knot at the end of the thread.

- Starting at one corner, sew one pinned edge together with small overhand stitches, removing the pins as you go. Sew the other pinned edge.

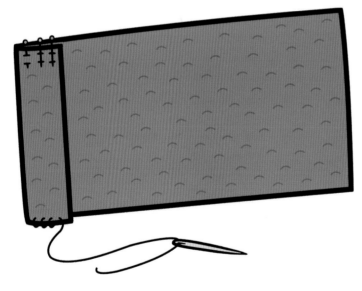

- Repeat to make a pocket at the other end of the cover.

TO EMBROIDER

- To embroider the ball of yarn, place the drinking glass in the center of the front cover and trace around it with a pencil or pen.

- Cut a piece of leftover yarn about as long as your arm. Thread the yarn needle and tie a knot about 2.5 cm (1 in.) from the yarn end.

- From the inside of the front cover, poke the needle up along the circle you traced. Sew small stitches around the edge of the circle. Then, using long stitches, add the yarn strands. When you run out of yarn, make a knot close to the inside of the cover and trim, and then start with a new piece of yarn.

- For the needles, use small stitches, embroider each needle top and then each needle end.

- For the ties, cut a 30 cm (12 in.) piece of leftover yarn. Thread the yarn needle and tie a knot about 2.5 cm (1 in.) from the yarn end. From the inside of the front cover, poke the needle up just to the right of the yarn ball center. Remove the needle. Repeat on the back of the cover to make the other tie.

Knit Bit

This doesn't have to be just for keeping track of your yarn projects. Wouldn't it be wicked to cover your school binders, too? Just make the cover bigger to fit the size of your binder.

Yarn girl project bag

You'll be right on target with a tote for all your project stuffs!
Since it's lined with a T-shirt, your needles won't poke through.

✱ *Note: You'll find the knitting chart on page 70.*

BAG

- With fuchsia yarn, CO 42 sts.

- Knit four rows in garter stitch (g st, see page 69).

- Beginning and ending with a purl row, knit 40 cm (16 in.) in stockinette stitch (St st, see page 69).

- Following the chart, knit the target pattern in St st.

- With fuchsia yarn, knit one row and then purl one row.

- Work four rows in g st.

- BO. Weave in the ends.

STRAP

- With fuchsia yarn, CO 7 sts.

- Work twelve rows in g st.

- Switch to orange yarn and work twelve rows in g st.

- Switch to light purple yarn and work twelve rows in g st.

- Repeat the fuchsia, orange and light purple stripes six more times.

- BO. Weave in the ends.

- Fold the strap in half lengthwise and pin.

- With yarn and a yarn needle, sew the strap into a tube by sewing the pinned edges together, removing the pins as you go.

ALL TOGETHER

- With WSF, fold the bag in half.

- Pin and then sew the sides together using yarn and a yarn needle, removing the pins as you go. Turn the bag right side out.

- Centering it over one side seam, and with the seam of the strap facing in, sew one end to the top edge of the bag. Repeat to sew the other end of the strap to the other side of the bag.

- Weave in the ends and trim.

T-SHIRT LINING

- Turn the T-shirt inside out and lay it flat.

- From the bottom left corner, measure across 28 cm (11 in.) and make a mark. From the same corner, measure up the side seam 31 cm (12¼ in.) and make a mark. Measure across 28 cm (11 in.) from this point and make another mark. Join the marks with straight lines and cut out the rectangle.

- Pin and then sew the cut edges with a seam that is 1 cm (½ in.) from the edges, removing the pins as you go.

- Tuck the lining into the bag with the open edges up. Pin and then sew around the open edges, removing the pins as you go.

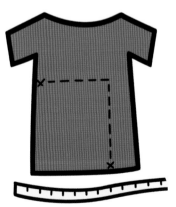

Knit Bit

When you're working the target pattern chart, make a few small balls of yarn for each of the different-colored sections: three orange, two light purple and six fuchsia.

Needle roll

Tuck your needles into a snug — and sublime — needle roll and you'll always know where to find them!

- Measure, mark and cut a 98 cm x 75 cm (39 in. x 30 in.) piece of fabric.

- Lay the fabric WSF. Fold one short edge over 2.5 cm (1 in.) and pin.

- Sew a seam along the pinned edge, 1 cm (½ in.) from the fold, removing the pins as you go.

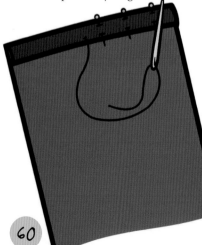

- Lay the fabric RSF. Measure and mark 23 cm (9 in.) along each side of the fabric from the sewn edge. Fold the fabric at the marks and pin along the edges.

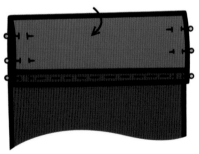

- Measure and mark 25 cm (10 in.) along each side of the fabric from the unsewn edge. Fold the fabric at the marks, overlapping the sewn edge, and pin along the edges.

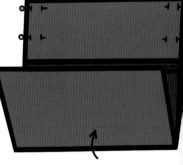

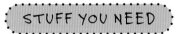

- 1 m (1 yd.) of denim or other fabric
- a sewing machine, or a sewing needle
- thread to match the fabric
- an iron and an ironing board
- one ball chunky weight yarn to match the fabric
- 6.5 mm (U.S. 10½) knitting needles
- a ruler or measuring tape, a pencil, scissors, pins

Add some knockout style to your knitting needles and then keep them in fine form with this sweet needle roll.

- Sew a 1 cm (½ in.) seam along the pinned edges, removing the pins as you go.

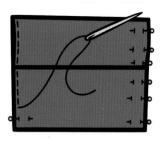

- Turn the roll right side out. Ask for an adult's help to iron the roll to flatten the seams.

- To make the needle pockets, lay the roll down with the open edge up. Measure and mark a line 5 cm (2 in.) from the left edge. Pin and then sew a seam along this line. Repeat four times to make four more pockets.

- Next, measure and mark a line 4 cm (1½ in.) from the last pocket. Pin and then sew a seam along this line. Repeat six times to make six more pockets this size.

- Then, measure and mark a line 2.5 cm (1 in.) from the last pocket. Pin and then sew a seam along this line. Repeat seven times to make seven more pockets this size.

TIE

- CO 3 sts.

- Work 60 cm (24 in.) in garter stitch (g st, see page 69). BO.

- Fold the tie in half. Pin, and then with a needle and thread sew the folded edge to the middle of the left edge of the roll.

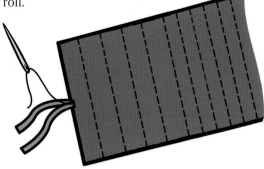

Nifty needles

*Knitting is an awesome way to show your unique style,
so why not add your creativity to your needles, too?*

BEADED NEEDLES

• If the needle tops are
  varnished or shiny, use a
  little sandpaper to sand the
  shine off, then wipe them
  clean with a damp cloth.

• Dip the needle tops into the Mod Podge, coating them
  evenly and tapping off any extra.

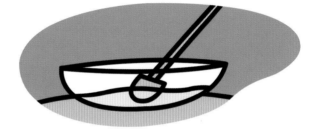

• Roll the needle tops into a small container of seed beads
  until they're completely covered. Let dry.

KNITTY NEEDLE COZY

STUFF YOU NEED

- knitting needles, any size
- leftover scraps of yarn (DK weight)
- 4 mm (U.S. 6) knitting needles
- two cotton balls, or some polyester filling/stuffing
- a ruler or measuring tape, scissors, a yarn needle

Gauge: 22 sts and 28 rows = 10 cm x 10 cm (4 in. x 4 in.)

- CO 6 sts.

- Starting with a purl row, work 13 rows in stockinette stitch (St st, see page 69).

- BO.

- Thread one of the yarn ends onto the yarn needle. Using duplicate stitch (see page 73), sew the short ends together to make a tube.

- Thread the yarn needle with one of the yarn ends. Put the top of the needle into the cozy and sew it closed below. Tuck a cotton ball in the top of the cozy and sew it closed. Weave in the ends and trim. Repeat for the other needle.

Knit Bit

Why not put little pics of your friends on your needle tops? Use a color copy or print a fab photo onto plain paper. Press a Page Pebble onto the picture and trim around the picture. With a glue gun, stick the Page Pebble onto a knitting needle with a flat round top.

Woolly Ways

Check out this section for tips, tricks and some basic stuff to help you out with knitting, crocheting and a couple types of felting. Look ahead for

knit knack and crochet play-by-play, including the basics

lists of abbreviations that you'll find in the projects

a guide to felting how-to

a couple of handy stitches for sewing knitted stuff together, and decorating, too!

The knitty gritty

Become a knit-wit with the basics of knitting in a nutshell.

CASTING ON

There are a few different ways to cast on (CO), but we'll just focus on one, the **continental** or **long-tail cast on**.

1. Pull out a strand of yarn from the ball, the "long tail," and make a slipknot. You'll need a shorter tail for smaller projects and a longer tail for larger projects.

2. Hold a knitting needle in your right hand. Slide the slipknot loop onto it so that the yarn attached to the ball is closest to you and the tail is away from you.

3. Press your left index finger and thumb together. Poke them between the two yarn strands and spread your finger and thumb apart. The tail should hang over your index finger and the yarn should hang over your thumb.

4. Catch the tail and the yarn in your palm with your other three fingers.

5. Poke the needle up through the loop that is around your thumb. Then, wrap the needle over and under the strand in front of your index finger. Pull the needle back out through the loop around your thumb.

6. Pull the new stitch snug on the needle. Repeat to make as many stitches as you need, counting the slipknot stitch as one.

Stitches

Anything you will ever knit will be made up of only two stitches, knit and purl, and different combos of the two:

KNIT (k)

1. Hold the needle with the stitches on it in your left hand and the empty needle in your right hand. Make sure the yarn is at the back of your work (away from you) and hold it in your right hand as well.

2. Poke the right needle into the first stitch, sliding it behind the left needle.

3. Wrap the yarn counter-clockwise around the end of the right needle.

4. Pull the yarn through the loop with the right needle to make a new stitch on the right needle.

5. Pull the old stitch off the left needle.

6. Repeat on the rest of the stitches on the left needle.

7. To start a new row, turn your work, put the right needle in your left hand and start again.

PURL (p)

1. Hold the needle with the stitches on it in your left hand and the empty needle in your right hand. Make sure the yarn is at the front of your work (closest to you) and hold it in your right hand as well.

2. Poke the right needle into the first stitch, sliding it in front of the left needle.

3. Wrap the yarn counter-clockwise around the end of the right needle.

4. Pull the yarn through the loop with the right needle to make a new stitch on the right needle.

5. Pull the old stitch off the left needle.

6. Repeat on the rest of the stitches on the left needle.

7. To start a new row, turn your work, put the right needle in your left hand and start again.

STOCKINETTE STITCH (St st)

Knit one row and then purl the next row. Alternate between knitting and purling the rows.

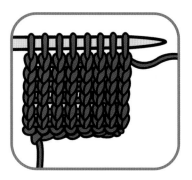

GARTER STITCH (g st)

Knit all rows with knit stitches.

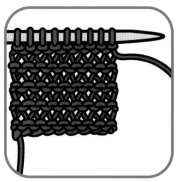

REPEAT FROM * TO *

Repeat the instructions that are in between the two asterisks (*) as many times as required.

DECREASING

There are two ways to decrease, or reduce, the number of stitches you're working with.

Method 1: To knit two stitches together (k2tog), poke the right needle through the next two stitches on the left needle at the same time. Knit them as you would knit one stitch.

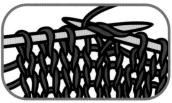

To decrease on a purl row, purl two stitches together (p2tog), poking the right needle through the next two stitches on the left needle at the same time. Purl them as you would purl one stitch.

Method 2: To slip and pass over one stitch, first slip one stitch (sl), insert the right needle into a stitch on the left needle, but instead of knitting it, just slide it off the left needle onto the right one.

Then knit one stitch and pass the slipped stitch over this stitch and off the needle (psso).

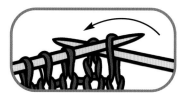

INCREASING

To increase the number of stitches you're working with for the projects in this book, you knit through the front and back of a loop (kf&b).

Knit into a stitch but don't take it off the left needle. Bring the point of the right needle around and insert it into the back of the same stitch.

Knit the stitch and take it off the left needle. You should have two stitches on the right needle.

KNITTING CHARTS

When you're knitting a design, like the target pattern on the Yarn Girl Project Bag (page 58), each chart square equals one stitch of your knitting. Start at the bottom of the chart. Follow the chart from right to left on knit rows and, on purl rows, follow it from left to right. To keep track of where you are, move a ruler or a sticky note up the chart as you go.

YARN SWITCHING

To switch yarn colors or to start a new ball, simply start knitting with the new yarn, leaving a 15 cm (6 in.) tail to weave in later. It's easiest to switch at the beginning of a row.

When you have many color changes in one row, make a few small balls of each color you need and add one whenever the new color starts.

Overlap the yarns when you switch from one ball to another so you don't get gaps in your knitting.

When you finish using one color, leave a 15 cm (6 in.) tail to weave in later.

Fixing Mistakes

The best way to fix a mistake is to undo the knitting until you get back to it and then start again. You can pull the knitting off the needle, unravel it to the mistake, and then put the stitches back on the needle. Or, for mistakes that are in the same row that you are on, you can unknit or "tink" them! Tink is "knit" spelled backward, and it means that you unknit the stitches by inserting the left needle back into the loop below the first stitch on the right needle.

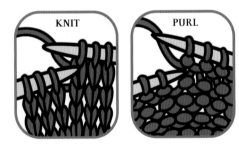

Bring the loop onto the left needle and pull the yarn to take out the old stitch.

Keep going until you are back where you need to be.

Binding off

Binding off (BO) is how you finish your knitted piece.

1. On the last row, knit the first two stitches. Then, with the tip of your left needle, pull the first stitch up and over the second stitch and off the needle. You should have one stitch on the right needle.

2. Knit another stitch and pull the second stitch over the third and off the needle. Keep going until you have no stitches on the left needle and only one stitch left on the right needle.

3. Leaving a 30 cm (12 in.) tail, cut the yarn. Draw the tail through the last stitch and take it off the needle. Pull the tail to close the last stitch.

Duplicate stitch

This is a type of embroidery that you do on the right side of a piece of knitting. The stitch copies, or duplicates, the knitted stitch, and it's great for adding a colorful design, your initial or, if you do it in the same color as your work, for hiding mistakes! Thread a yarn needle with a piece of yarn. From the wrong side of the knitting, poke the needle up through the bottom V of a stitch.

Sew under the two strands at the top of the stitch, and then back down through the V again.

Finishing and blocking

Once you've finished a knitted piece, use a yarn needle to weave in all the tail ends into the back of the work for a few centimeters (inches) like this.

Trim off the remaining yarn ends close to the knitting.

To sew knitted pieces together, thread a yarn needle with a piece of yarn as long as your arm. Pin the pieces together along the seam to be sewn. Sew the pieces together by weaving the needle back and forth, under the stitches next to the edge.

When done, remove the pins, and weave in and trim the yarn ends.

Blocking is a way to make your finished work look tidy. Lay a finished piece of knitting on an ironing board with a thin piece of cloth on top. Ask an adult to help you use the steam surge button to iron it gently one section at a time until it is smooth. Let cool.

Crochet play-by-play

Crochet (sounds like crow-shay!) is super fun—and easy to do.

STITCHES

CHAIN STITCH (ch)

Use a chain stitch to start a crochet project.

1. Make a slipknot, leaving a 30 cm (12 in.) tail.

2. Poke the crochet hook into the slipknot loop, hook the yarn and pull it through to make another loop. Repeat to make as many chain stitches as you need for the foundation row.

Knit Bit

A chain stitch is also used for moving from one row to another. If the next row is single crochet, chain 1 stitch before turning your work to start the new row. If the next row is double crochet, chain 3 stitches before turning.

SINGLE CROCHET (sc)

1. For the first row of a project, insert the hook into the second chain from the hook on the foundation row, wrap the yarn over the hook and pull the loop back through the chain.

2. You should have two loops on your hook. Wrap the yarn over the hook again and pull it through both loops.

3. Continue along the chain stitches in the foundation row to the end, but don't crochet into the slipknot. Count your stitches to make sure you have the right number.

4. To single crochet into a row after the first one, chain one stitch, turn your work around and insert your hook under both loops of the first stitch.

5. Finish the single crochet stitch the same way you did on the foundation row, by wrapping the yarn over the hook again and pulling it through both loops.

DOUBLE CROCHET (dc)

1. For the project's first row, wrap the yarn over the hook and insert the hook into the fourth chain from the hook on the foundation row.

2. Then, wrap the yarn over the hook and pull the loop back through the chain. You should have three loops on your hook.

3. Wrap the yarn over the hook again. Pull it through the first two loops on the hook. Wrap the yarn over the hook again and pull it through both loops.

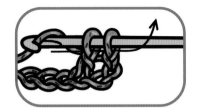

4. Continue along the chain stitches in the foundation row to the end, but don't crochet into the slipknot. Count your stitches to make sure you have the right number.

5. To double crochet into a row after the first one, chain three stitches, turn your work around and insert your hook under both loops of the second stitch.

6. Finish the double crochet stitch the same way you did on the foundation row, by wrapping the yarn over the hook again and pulling it through the first two loops on the hook.

CROCHETING IN ROWS OR ROUNDS

When you crochet in rows, you simply go back and forth along a row. When you get to the end of one row, you make some chains before you turn your work to start the next row. The number of chains depends on the stitch you're using. If the next row is single crochet, chain one before you turn and begin the next row. If the next row is double crochet, chain three before you turn.

When you crochet in rounds, you are going around in a circle. Be sure to use a stitch marker to mark the beginning of each round so that you'll always know where you began. Also, when you're going to take a break, it's a good idea to stop at the end of a round so that you don't lose count.

SLIP STITCH

For the projects in this book, you close each round by joining the first and last stitches in the round with a slip stitch.

1. Poke the hook through the first stitch in the round.

2. Hook the yarn and pull it through the two loops on the hook.

3. Start a new round by chaining as you would for a new row.

FASTENING OFF

Fastening off is how you finish your crocheted piece.

1. When you only have one loop left on the hook, leave a 30 cm (12 in.) tail and cut the yarn.

2. Draw the tail through the last loop and pull the tail to close it.

FINISHING AND BLOCKING

Follow the instructions for knitted pieces on page 73.

Taking care of your wares

Once you've spent time working on a project, you'll want to make sure that it stays nice looking. Read and follow the care instructions on the yarn label. As a general rule, though, never put a knitted or crocheted item in the washing machine, especially if it's made from natural fibers (unless you want to felt it!). Handwash your project with a mild detergent, then rinse and gently squeeze out the water without wringing it. Lay it flat to dry.

Fab felting

Felting is the process of taking wool fiber or something knitted and making it matted and dense. Sounds a bit like a boo-boo, huh? So, why would you want to do this?! Because it looks super cool, it's really strong and durable — and, if you're felting something you knitted, it's great for hiding mistakes!

WOOL FIBER FELTING

Wool fiber, sometimes called roving, is what yarn is spun from. You can buy it at a yarn shop — but sometimes it's tucked away, so you might have to ask for it. It comes in lots of great colors and looks a lot like cotton. There are two ways to felt it: with needles or with soapy water.

NEEDLE FELTING

You'll need a set of needle-felting needles, which you can get where you get the wool fiber. These are very sharp, so make sure to keep them pointed away from you and definitely wear some gloves to protect your hands.

1. Protect your work surface with a mat or some newspaper, and then put a piece of foam under your work. This will give the needles something to poke into.

2. Next, cut a piece of polyester felt to the size you want your project to be for the background.

3. Then, lay down pieces of wool fiber that are about 2.5 to 3 cm (1 to 2 in.) thick.

4. To felt the wool fiber onto the background polyester felt, poke a felting needle into the wool fiber a whole bunch of times, until it becomes matted and dense and forms one piece of felted material.

If you have more than one size of felting needle, you can start with a thicker one and then move to a thinner one as the wool becomes more felted. You can add more colors of wool fiber to make a design by laying the pieces down in any shape you like and then felting them in place.

SOAPY WATER FELTING

All you need to make felted balls from wool fiber is — you guessed it! — soapy water.

1. Tear off a small amount of wool fiber, enough to roll into a small ball.

2. Put a little dish soap in a bowl and fill it halfway with hot tap water.

3. Wearing rubber gloves, soak the ball in the hot, sudsy water. Take it out of the water and roll it in your palms vigorously. Soak it again and continue rolling. After a few soak-and-rolls, run the ball under cold water. Continue till it's firm and smooth.

4. Run the ball under cold water again, then gently squeeze out some of the water. Set it on a towel to dry.

You can use this technique to make any size of ball — just start with a bigger ball of wool fiber. Also, you can mix in different colors as you go to make striped or spotty balls.

79

FELTING STUFF IN A WASHING MACHINE

You can felt knitted or crocheted stuff, but it has to be made from 100% real wool. Synthetic yarns don't felt at all. Put your knitted thing into a mesh laundry bag. Fill the washing machine with hot water to the lowest water level and set the speed to heavy duty. Add a small amount of detergent — 15 to 30 ml (1 to 2 tbsp.) — and add the knitted thing and an old towel to help it agitate. Let the machine agitate, checking every few minutes to see how felted the knitted thing is and what size it is.

It's really important to do this because it's easy to shrink your knitted thing too much, and there's no way to unshrink it!

Once your knitted thing is felted to the right size, take it out of the machine (don't let it go to rinse cycle).

Rinse it under cool water and roll it in a towel. Gently squeeze the water out, but don't wring it. Lay it on a dry towel and measure and adjust it to the right size and shape by gently pulling the edges, if needed. Let dry.

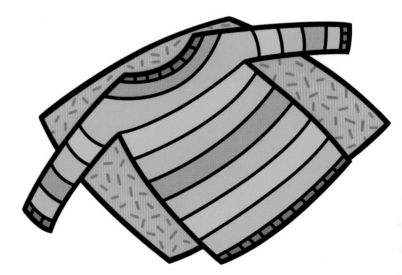